HOLY CITIES

AMRITSAR

Beryl Dhanjal

Evans

Evans Brothers Limited

Published by Evans Brothers Limited
2A Portman Mansions
Chiltern Street
London W1M 1LE

© copyright in the text and illustrations
Evans Brothers Limited 1994

First published 1994

Printed in Hong Kong by Wing King Tong Co. Ltd.

ISBN 0 237 51253 X

ACKNOWLEDGEMENTS

Editorial: Catherine Chambers and Jean Coppendale
Design: Monica Chia
Production: Jenny Mulvanny

Maps: Jillian Luff of Bitmap Graphics

The author and publishers would like to thank:
Saviour Pirotta for his help in devising the Holy
Cities series.

Eleanor Nesbitt for all her valuable help and advice.

For permission to reproduce copyright material the author
and publishers gratefully acknowledge the following:

Front cover: Main photograph – The pool and the
Harmandir; inset left – A Nihang warrior. Nihangs date
back to the 18th century. They were known for their
fierceness and their courage; inset right – Part of a patterned
wall inside the Golden Temple

Back cover: Looking over a balcony in the Golden Temple

Endpapers: Front – Gold and glass on the first floor of the
Harmandir; back – the Harmandir at night

Title page: A fresco showing Guru Nanak, the first Guru

Contents page: A pattern on the wall of the first floor of the
Golden Temple

All the photographs in this book have been reproduced with
the permission of Helene Rogers/Trip, with the exception of
page 12 – (bottom right) Phil and Val Emmett; page 36 –
(top) Ann and Bury Peerless, (bottom) Liba Taylor, The
Hutchison Library; page 37 – (top) Phil and Val Emmett,
(bottom) Liba Taylor, The Hutchison Library; page 38 – (top)
Ann and Bury Peerless, (bottom) The Hutchison Library;
page 39 – Liba Taylor, The Hutchison Library.

Contents

The meanings of the words in **bold** can be found in the **Key words** sections at the end of each chapter.

Introduction

Amritsar is the most sacred city for the world's 16 million Sikhs. It lies in the State of Panjab in north-west India, where Sikhism was born. The city rests on a large, flat plain which reaches across into Pakistan to the north, where it rises into the Himalaya and Karakoram mountains. Five rivers cut across the fertile land. They give both the area and the state the name Panjab, for in the Panjabi language, *panj* means 'five', and in Persian, *ab* means 'water'. Panjabi is the language spoken by most Sikhs, and an old form is also used in their holy **scriptures**.

The most striking image of Amritsar is its enormous pool, with the magnificent Golden Temple shining in the centre. The name Amritsar means 'pool of nectar', and its waters are said to bring **immortality** to those who bathe in them. But it is not only these sacred waters that make the city special for Sikhs. For inside the Golden Temple lies the collection of Sikh holy scriptures known as the **Guru** Granth Sahib.

Pilgrims walking across the bridge to the Golden Temple.

Amritsar was built as a holy city during the 1570s by Guru Ram Das, the fourth of the ten Gurus who developed Sikhism. Since then, Amritsar has undergone many changes and has been demolished and rebuilt several times. Today it is a lively, modern city, and although Sikhs do not have to go on **pilgrimage**, they come from all over the world to visit the Golden Temple, the many **shrines**, and to walk around the sacred pool on patterned marble pavements.

Key words

scriptures holy writings

immortality everlasting life, of the spirit

Guru teacher

pilgrimage a visit to a holy place

shrines special places where a holy person had lived or visited, or is buried

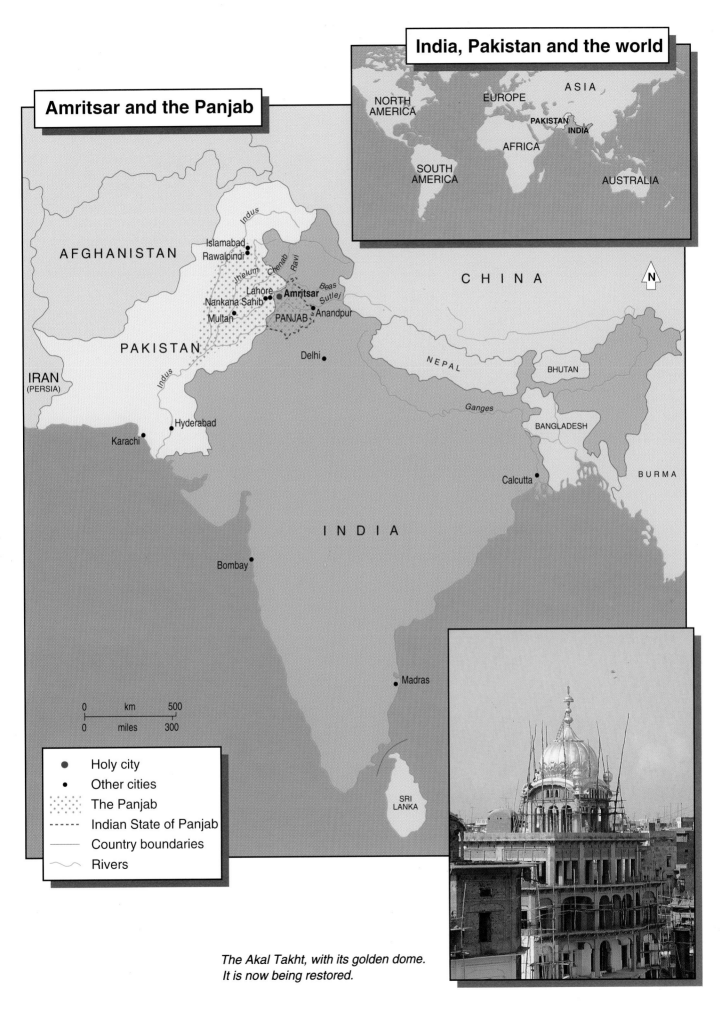

Amritsar and the Panjab

India, Pakistan and the world

NORTH
AMERICA

EUROPE

ASIA

PAKISTAN

INDIA

AFRICA

SOUTH
AMERICA

AUSTRALIA

AFGHANISTAN

Indus

Islamabad
Rawalpindi

Jhelum

Chenab

Ravi

C H I N A

N

IRAN
(PERSIA)

PAKISTAN

Lahore
Nankana Sahib

Multan

Indus

Beas

Amritsar

Sutlej

PANJAB · Anandpur

Delhi

N E P A L

BHUTAN

Ganges

BANGLADESH

BURMA

Hyderabad

Karachi

Calcutta

I N D I A

Bombay

| 0 | km | 500 |
| 0 | miles | 300 |

Madras

- Holy city
- Other cities
- The Panjab
- - - Indian State of Panjab
— Country boundaries
〜 Rivers

SRI
LANKA

The Akal Takht, with its golden dome.
It is now being restored.

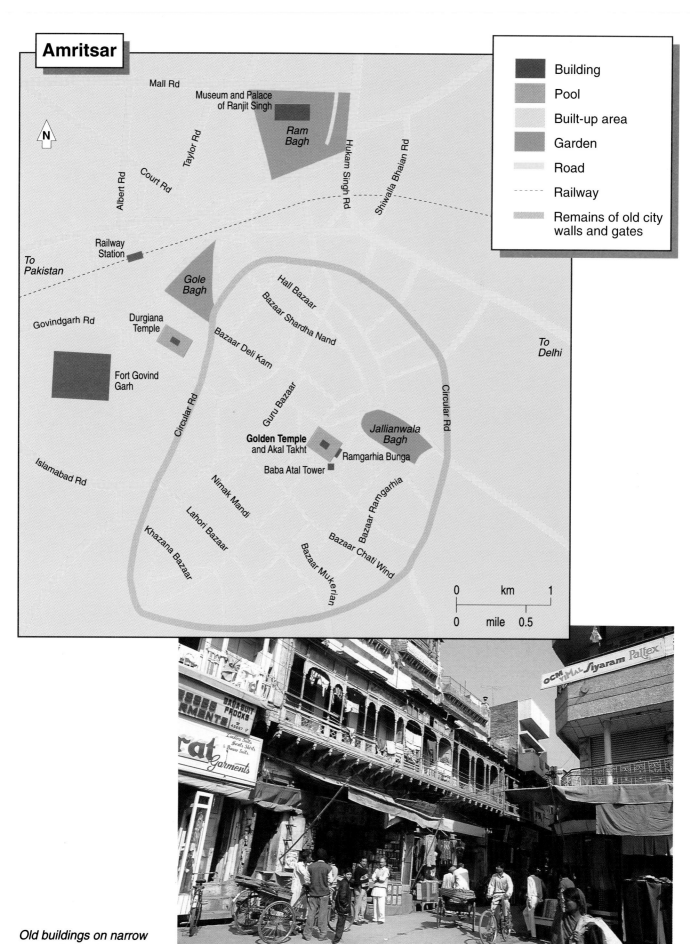

Amritsar

Legend:
- Building
- Pool
- Built-up area
- Garden
- Road
- Railway
- Remains of old city walls and gates

Mall Rd

Museum and Palace of Ranjit Singh

Ram Bagh

N

Taylor Rd

Court Rd

Albert Rd

Hukam Singh Rd

Shiwalla Bhaian Rd

Railway Station

To Pakistan

Gole Bagh

Hall Bazaar

Bazaar Shardha Nand

Govindgarh Rd

Durgiana Temple

Bazaar Deli Kam

To Delhi

Fort Govind Garh

Guru Bazaar

Circular Rd

Golden Temple and Akal Takht

Jallianwala Bagh

Ramgarhia Bunga

Islamabad Rd

Baba Atal Tower

Circular Rd

Nimak Mandi

Bazaar Ramgarhia

Lahori Bazaar

Bazaar Chati Wind

Khazana Bazaar

Bazaar Mukerian

0   km   1

0   mile   0.5

Old buildings on narrow streets in Amritsar.

The Gurus and their teachings

The first Guru

The first teacher and founder of the Sikh religion was Guru Nanak, who was born in 1469 at a place called Nankana Sahib. Nankana Sahib is not far from Lahore, which is now in Pakistan, but only about 55 kilometres from Amritsar. Guru Nanak was born into a **Hindu** family, although at this time, **Muslims** ruled the Panjab. Hinduism and Islam (the Muslim religion) did not always exist happily together.

When Guru Nanak was born, traditional stories tell of miraculous signs which showed that a very special person had arrived. There were many miracles associated with his childhood. In one of them, Nanak was supposed to be looking after his father's buffaloes when he fell asleep. The buffaloes wrecked a neighbour's field. But when an official arrived to see how much damage had been done, the field seemed quite normal again.

◀ *Guru Nanak surrounded by the other nine Gurus. Below his beard is a copy of the Guru Granth Sahib, covered in cloths (see page 22).*

In Sikh tradition, Guru Nanak saves the Muslim musician,
▼ *Mardana, from being boiled alive by a demon.*

When the Guru was a young man he had a strange experience. Traditional stories say that he was transported to the Court of God, where he was told to go out and teach God's message. Guru Nanak travelled around India accompanied by a Muslim musician called Mardana and a Hindu called Bala. The Guru often sang hymns and verse as part of his teachings. Music is still an important part of Sikh worship today.

Guru Nanak's teachings

Guru Nanak taught that people should remember the Name of God, because the Name is all that we can say about Him and and all that we know of Him. We should **meditate** on His qualities and live according to His laws, which are the laws of our universe. Then, if God wishes, we shall become united with Him. This is not like going to heaven; it is a kind of peace and harmony which we experience whilst we are still alive.

Guru Nanak believed that the religion which really matters is the truth inside our hearts. He taught that truth and goodness should be a part of everyday life, and that Sikhs should lead ordinary lives. Guru Nanak did not believe in complicated **rituals**, worshipping images, or going on pilgrimages. One of his most important teachings was that God matters more than any religious ceremony.

Guru Nanak attracted many followers. In Panjabi, the word for followers is 'Sikhs'. The Guru was loved by all and when he died, it is said that both Hindus and Muslims claimed him as their own. Guru Nanak treated Hindus and Muslims as equals, even though his own beliefs were different.

The last Guru

Before Guru Nanak died he asked Guru Angad to take over from him. Altogether there were ten Sikh Gurus. Many of them developed towns and it was the fourth Guru, Ram Das, who started to build the holy city of Amritsar (see page 13). The last Guru, Govind Singh, died in 1708. Thereafter, leadership of the Sikh community was given to the Gurus' holy writings, which are called Guru Granth Sahib (see pages 20 to 22). The first Guru Granth Sahib was placed in the Harmandir in Amritsar by the fifth Guru, Arjan.

At first, Gurus were peaceful holy men who loved God and expressed their ideas through beautiful poetry. Later, though, Gurus were more like princes whose rule became increasingly political.

Guru Ram Das

The Gurus

Nanak became Guru in 1499. Each new Guru took over the leadership of the Sikh community after the death of the previous Guru.

	YEAR OF BIRTH	YEAR OF DEATH
Guru Nanak	(1469–1539)	
Guru Angad	(1504–1552)	
Guru Amar Das	(1479–1574)	
Guru Ram Das	(1534–1581)	
Guru Arjan	(1563–1606)	
Guru Hargovind	(1595–1644)	
Guru Har Rai	(1630–1661)	
Guru Har Krishan	(1656–1664)	
Guru Tegh Bahadur	(1621–1675)	
Guru Govind Singh	(1666–1708)	

The Khalsa

In 1699, Guru Govind Singh called his followers together at a town called Anandpur. He founded a special group of people called the Khalsa, which is usually translated as 'pure'. The first five members of the Guru's Khalsa were known as the *Panj Piare* – the 'five loved ones'.

The Guru laid down rules by which these chosen Sikhs were to live. To identify the members of the Khalsa he gave them five special things to wear. These are known as the *Panj Kakke*, or the 'Five Ks', as each item begins with the letter 'k'.

Today, both men and women can become members of the Khalsa, just as they can both

A picture of Guru Govind Singh on the back of a lorry in Amritsar. Pictures of the Gurus can be seen all over Amritsar.

read and take care of the Guru Granth Sahib (see page 22). Before becoming a member of the Khalsa, a Sikh has to promise to obey Sikh rules, just as the first *Panj Piare* did. Like the first members, they have to drink *amrit*, the holy nectar, or water of life. This is made of sugar and water and is stirred in a bowl with a sword. The sugar dissolves in the water just as the divisions between human beings should dissolve. Sikhs believe that in God's eyes we are all equal and should act together in unity.

The Khalsa symbols – *Panj Kakke*

Kes   A beard, and uncut hair that is covered by a turban. It is a symbol of acceptance of God's gifts.

Kangha   A wooden comb for keeping the Kes tidy. It is a symbol of discipline.

Kara   A steel bracelet worn on the right wrist. It is a symbol of unity.

Kirpan   A small sword. It is a symbol of justice and spiritual power.

Kachh   Shorts, traditionally worn by soldiers. They are a symbol of readiness for action.

Karas *(steel bracelets) on sale in Amritsar.*

A turban shop in Amritsar. The turban is not one of the Five Ks, but many Sikh men wear one to cover the Kes.

Key words

Hindu following the Hindu religion, which developed in India from about 4,000 years ago

Muslims   followers of Islam, the religion brought into India 1300 years ago

meditate   think deeply

rituals   religious ceremony

A member of the Khalsa wearing the Five Ks at a ceremony in Britain.

The founding of Amritsar

Between 1526 and 1858, while India was under Muslim rule, the Sikh Gurus established many towns, including Amritsar. One tradition says that the land on which Amritsar was built was given to the third Guru, Amar Das, by the Muslim ruler, Emperor Akbar. No one knows if this is true but it was certainly Amar Das who established the site of Amritsar, close to a natural pool that was said to contain healing waters.

The pool of miracles

There are many Sikh legends and traditions linked with the site of Amritsar and especially with the pool (see pages 34 to 35). It is said that there was always an *amritkund*, a reservoir of the nectar of immortality, where Amritsar now stands. Stories of these waters are told not only in Sikh tradition but also in the traditions of other Indian religions.

It is said that the Hindu god, Ram, and his sons fought at the holy site of Amritsar. Ram was killed and then miraculously healed when he was given the *amrit* (nectar) to drink. Some people say that the Lord Buddha, founder of the Buddhist religion, also visited the pool. But Sikhs believe that Guru Amar Das cured the second Guru, Angad, of a skin disease by using a herb that grew near the pond. The site of Amritsar was certainly very special to people of many different faiths.

Who will build the holy city?

Guru Amar Das did not build Amritsar himself. This was left to his son-in-law, the fourth Guru, Ram Das. It is said that Guru Amar Das tested Ram Das and another son-in-law to see which one of them would be the most worthy Guru to follow after him. The Guru challenged each man to build a raised platform, to see which was the best. After the platforms had been completed, the Guru then told his sons-in-law that the platforms were not good enough. He ordered the two men to pull them down. The other son-in-law became very angry and refused to do as he was asked, but Ram Das knocked down his own platform without protest.

Ram Das was tested even further. He had to rebuild the platform seven times before the Guru was satisfied. Guru Amar Das then proclaimed that seven more generations of Gurus would occupy the throne of the Guru. After that, Sikhs would have no human leader.

Ram Das makes the pools

From building seven platforms, Ram Das went on to build the holy city of Amritsar. He developed the site with the help of a group of elderly and well respected Sikhs. First, the Guru had a new pool excavated. This pool was called Santokhsar, after a Sikh follower called Santokha of Peshawar. *Santokh* means 'contentment'. But before the pool was even finished and paved, the Guru asked Ram Das to build another pool on low-lying ground to the east of the first one. This was to be the Amritsar, the pool of nectar that gives immortality.

A **jujube** tree called Dukhbanjani Ber marked the spot where the pool was to be made. It is still there today. Labourers were hired to dig the pool but many Sikh followers helped out. As the pool progressed, traders and businessmen were drawn to the settlement to serve the workmen's needs. Wells were dug, homes were built and markets were set up. A small town was beginning to grow. Guru Amar Das died in 1574. Ram Das became the fourth Guru and completed the pools in 1577.

Dukhbanjani Ber, by the sacred pool.

The temple in the pool

In 1581, Arjan became Guru and decided to have the holy pool lined with bricks. A temple was to be built in the middle of it. The story of the first temple has attracted many legends. Sikh tradition says that it was designed by the Guru himself. It was also thought that he laid the foundation stone. But most people now believe that it was laid by Mian Mir, a Muslim saint from Lahore.

It is said that when the stone was put down, it was crooked. A stonemason straightened it but the saint said that it was a pity he had done so. If the stone had remained as he had put it, then the temple would have remained forever. As it was, the temple would need to be rebuilt in the future. The saint was right; the temple was demolished and rebuilt three times. It is now known throughout the world as the Golden Temple. But Sikhs call it Darbar Sahib, the Lord's Court, or Harmandir Sahib, God's Temple.

The Akal Takht

Under Guru Arjan, Amritsar grew and prospered. New houses were built and bathing pools and gardens were laid out. But Guru Arjan's life ended tragically. There were problems with the Muslim emperor, Jehangir, and the Guru was executed in Lahore in 1606. He was one of many Sikh **martyrs**.

The death of Guru Arjan changed Sikhism in Amritsar. The sixth Guru was Guru Arjan's son, Hargovind. He now felt the need to defend his faith and build a strong Sikh community. Guru Hargovind wore two swords: one represented his spiritual power and the other his worldly authority. He was not only a holy man as the other Gurus had been; he was also a prince.

This change in Sikhism led to new developments in Amritsar. A raised platform with a building on top was put up about 80 metres from the Harmandir. It was called the Akal Takht, the Throne of the Timeless One. Inside the new building, Guru Hargovind set

The Akal Takht, with its golden dome. It is now being rebuilt following damage caused in 1984 (see page 17).

up a court of justice and a team of administrators. Decisions and orders were sent out to the community from the Akal Takht, as they still are today.

But the strength of Guru Hargovind led to conflict with the Muslim rulers, so he moved away from Amritsar. Guru Hargovind was the last Guru to have direct links with Amritsar; the next four Gurus lived elsewhere. The last Guru of all, Govind Singh, made sure that his trusted friend, Bhai Mani Singh, took control over the affairs of the Harmandir. When the Guru died in 1708, Bhai Mani Singh passed the authority of the Guru to the Sikh holy scriptures, the Guru Granth Sahib, as Guru Govind Singh had wanted.

Key words

jujube a small, thorny fruit tree

martyrs people who are killed because of their beliefs

Think and do

The pool and the Harmandir are associated with many miracles (see also the story on page 34). What is a miracle? Can you tell the story of a modern-day miracle?

After the Gurus

After the death of the last Guru, the Panjab suffered weak government by the Mughal emperors, invasions from Persia and Afghanistan, and a lot of devastation. At times, Amritsar was almost deserted. Sikhs became divided into groups called *misls*, each with their own warlord, known as a *misldar*. Two great leaders, Jassa Singh Ramgarhia, and Jassa Singh Ahluwalia, emerged. Jassa Singh Ramgarhia built a strong fort near Amritsar called Ram Gahr – God's Fort, from which Jassa Singh took his own name. These two mighty Sikh leaders helped to strengthen their people, and as the Muslim Mughal empire declined towards the end of the 18th century, a Sikh empire grew.

The growth of Amritsar

After many troubles, Amritsar slowly developed. By 1776, the pool, the Harmandir,

One of the Sikh heroes, Jassa Singh Ramgarhia.

the bridge and the gate, known as the Darshani Darwaza, had been completed. Other shrines were built around the pool.

The different groups of Sikhs built homes in Amritsar and put up their own small forts surrounded by defensive walls. These areas were called *katras*. Each one was named after

Ramgarhia Bunga still stands today. It was built right beside the sacred pool.

The large Mughal coronation slab that still lies in Ramgarhia Bunga.

its founder. Nowadays, a *katra* is a residential area with a market. *Katras* are special to Amritsar; other towns do not have them.

In 1794, Jassa Singh Ramgarhia built a large residence, called a *bunga*, near the Harmandir. It is a fine old building with two towers which rise to 46 metres. These towers were damaged in 1984 when Indian government troops accidentally struck the Harmandir area. There were originally four planned but only two were completed.

Jassa Singh had conquered territory as far afield as Delhi, where he removed the slab from the throne on which the Mughal coronation ceremonies were held. He took the slab back to Amritsar and placed it in the Ramgarhia Bunga where it still lies.

The *bungas* were originally used by Sikhs to prepare themselves for attacks on their city. But as the invasions stopped and Sikh power grew, the *bungas* and residences became more like royal courts. There was plenty of room for visitors and pilgrims to stay. Each *misl* had his own *bunga*, and many rich and important people began to build them. Gradually, each community within the city had its own. There are said to have been more than 70 *bungas* by the early 19th century. Apart from the Ramgarhia Bunga, all of them have now been pulled down to make way for modern buildings.

The old *bungas* were important centres of learning and art. They attracted scholars, writers, artists, musicians, doctors and **calligraphers.** Historians and **theologians** studied beside the pool and the temple. It was like a great university.

During the 20th century, the land on which the *bungas* were built was bought by the Shiromani Gurdwara Prabandhak Committee, which controls Sikh affairs. The *bungas* were demolished and the centre of learning vanished. **Frescoes** and other decorations were destroyed. The land was used to widen the *parakrama,* the pathway around the pool. A new meeting hall was built, a hospital, some hostels and offices, and a Guru's kitchen, where meals are prepared for worshippers (see page 27).

Ranjit Singh, the great builder

Maharaja Ranjit Singh was a great Sikh emperor who ruled in the Panjab between 1799 and 1839. He developed Amritsar more than anyone else. Amritsar as it is today was built largely by him.

In 1799, Ranjit Singh seized Lahore, then the capital of the Panjab. Soon after, he took Amritsar, which was still just a collection of *katras* and *bungas*. Each one was ruled by a different family, which kept its own defence force and employed its own tax collectors.

When Ranjit Singh took over the city he united it, demolished the small forts and built a massive city wall. It is said to have been 20 metres wide and 6 metres high, with a large moat all around it. There were 12 gates leading into the city. When the wall was finished, Ranjit Singh rode in triumph through Amritsar on an elephant, showering coins on the cheering crowds. He bathed in the sacred pool and gave money to have the Harmandir rebuilt in marble and covered in gold. The Harmandir then became known as the Golden Temple.

During Ranjit Singh's rule many more people built *bungas,* which were decorated with murals and mirror work. Some of them were very tall. A commercial centre grew, with markets for rice, dyes and fabrics, and for ironworkers and saddlers. There were gardens and open spaces all within the city wall. Carpenters, blacksmiths, ivory carvers, potters, shoemakers, weavers, goldsmiths, leatherworkers, dyers and gunsmiths all traded in the city. Clothmakers wove Pashmina shawls which are made of a special kind of wool. Shoemakers sewed *jhootis* – the richly embroidered shoes with curled toes. Metal crafts were very highly developed and Ranjit Singh had coins minted in the names of the Gurus.

Ranjit Singh's own palace was called the Rambagh. It was set in a beautiful garden which was laid out in 1819. Gardening was a great hobby with wealthy people in India. The design of Ranjit Singh's garden was greatly influenced by the Muslim Shalimar Gardens in Lahore. But there was a big wall and a moat around Ranjit Singh's, with ramparts and a gate with spaces for guns in it. In the centre, a palace with a cool underground chamber was built. A double row of fountains crossed the garden. The majestic palace showed the strength of Ranjit Singh's influence in Amritsar.

The British in Amritsar

Amritsar developed well during the rule of Ranjit Singh, but after he died there was no one else who was as strong and as capable as he was. The kingdom fell apart.

During the early 19th century, the British had gradually gained power in India to protect their trade in Asia. They had been trading in India since 1600. Panjab was the last territory which they took, in 1849. The British built government offices, roads and railways, so that law and order could be maintained and trade could carry on peacefully. They also made irrigation channels, which meant that more fields could be cultivated. Panjab grew richer.

Amritsar railway station.

MRITSAR.

The Golden Temple.

The Golden Temple with the clock tower which was built by the British.

A bungalow built for a British family living in Amritsar during the colonial period.

In Amritsar, the British built law courts, a hospital, a railway station, a town hall and district offices. They also built houses called bungalows – a word from India that has now become part of the English language. The British added to the Harmandir by building a clock tower near by, which the Sikhs demolished when they took control of the Golden Temple once more. The British remained in the Panjab for 100 years.

Key words

calligraphers artists who paint beautiful lettering

theologians people who study religion

frescoes wall paintings made on damp plaster

The Guru Granth Sahib

The teachings in the Guru Granth Sahib guide all Sikhs towards an understanding of God, who is the True Guru. They also show Sikhs how they should live in order to get close to Him. These teachings are called *Gurbani*, which means 'Words of the Guru'.

The Guru Granth Sahib is really a collection of religious poems which are sung. They are known as *shabads* and were written by the first five Gurus: Nanak, Angad, Amar Das, Ram Das and Arjan, by the ninth Guru, and by 36 other holy men from northern India. Some of the poems were written by Hindus and Muslims; some of the poets were rich and powerful, while others were poor and from humble families. Sikhs believe that people of all faiths and all walks of life are able to know the Word of God. Altogether there are 1430 pages of *shabads* in the book.

At first, there were separate books of poetry but Guru Arjan collected them together and took them to Amritsar to make them into a single book. They were brought to a place now called Ath Sath Tirath, which means 68 places of pilgrimage. It is a very sacred spot. People believe that one visit here is equal to visiting 68 pilgrimage sites spread across India.

When Guru Arjan reached Ath Sath Tirath, he called for his friend , Bhai Gurdas Bhalla, to help him put together the holy writings. The two of them sat beside a pool called Ramsar. Here, the Guru read aloud the poetry that was to be included in the book while Bhai Gurdas wrote it down. When the holy volume was ready it was placed in the centre of the Harmandir. Baba Buddha, a wise man and companion to many Gurus,

The Guru Granth Sahib being read near Ath Sath Tirath, where the scriptures were written down.

▲ The Guru Granth Sahib on the ground floor of the Golden Temple.

◄ Reading the Guru Granth Sahib on the first floor of the Harmandir. The script in which it is written is called Gurmukhi.

The Guru Granth Sahib today

Today, every Sikh temple has a Guru Granth Sahib. Some families also have one in their homes, although the book is very large and needs to be put in a room on its own to give it proper respect. Each Guru Granth Sahib has the same number of pages and the *shabads* are laid out in exactly the same way in every book.

In the Harmandir and in every *gurdwara*, the Guru Granth Sahib rests on a throne. In each place of worship the throne is made up in the same way, from a wooden base with cushions and richly decorated cloths laid on top of each other in a certain order. When the book is not being used it is covered with a cloth called a *rumala*.

Parts of the Guru Granth Sahib are read during worship at the *gurdwara*. A continuous 48-hour reading of the Guru Granth Sahib often takes place. This is called an *akhand path*, which means 'unbroken reading'. Readers take it in turns to recite the verses, each person reading aloud for no more than two hours at a time.

Chauris on sale in Amritsar. These are special fans which are waved over the Guru Granth Sahib as a sign of respect. Before the holy book was completed, the Gurus were fanned with a chauri by their followers.

was appointed as the first *granthi* (see page 11). *Granth* means 'book' and a *granthi* is a person who cares for the book. Today, in each Sikh community, a *granthi* looks after the *gurdwara* (temple), as well as the Guru Granth Sahib.

When Baba Buddha first opened the book in the Harmandir, the very first line which met his eyes was: 'The creator stood in the midst of the work.' To Baba Buddha, this meant that the book of poetry was the Word of God. From the 18th century, Sikhs began to use these words in their daily prayer:

> 'Accept the Guru Granth as the visible body of the Guru. Those whose hearts are pure can find truth (God) in the word.'

The Mool Mantra

This is the first hymn which was composed by Guru Nanak. It gives a good idea of the basic beliefs of Sikhism.

There is only one God

Whose name is Truth

The Creator

Without fear

Without hate

A timeless being who

does not take birth

Self existent

Known only by

the Guru's grace

A day at the Harmandir

▲ *Some pilgrims bathe in the sacred pool before they enter the Harmandir.*

▶ *Entering the doorway to the Harmandir.*

There are nearly always worshippers and pilgrims at the Harmandir. They arrive every day before the doors are opened, three hours before dawn at two or three o'clock in the morning. According to Sikh scriptures, this is a time for prayer. There is quiet early morning hymn singing until about five o'clock, when the preparations are made to receive the Guru Granth Sahib. The throne is ready and the holy book is carried in on a golden **palanquin**. Trumpeters and **conch** players lead the way to the first floor of the Harmandir. Here, the holy book is placed on the throne and unwrapped.

A *granthi* opens the book, without choosing a particular part, and reads out the verse from the top of the left-hand page. This verse is known as *waq* or *hukam*. It gives Sikhs their orders and guidance for the day. After the

verse has been read aloud, it is written down so that people who come for help later in the day can hear what was advised. The rest of the book is then read.

Then a special morning hymn by Guru Nanak is recited and worshippers follow with the *Ardas*, which means 'request'. The *Ardas* is a special Sikh prayer, most of it dating from the 18th century. It is the only prayer which is not taken from the Guru Granth Sahib. The *Ardas* allows people to say their own personal prayers.

After this, *karah prasad* is given out. This is sacred food, made in a special way (see page 27). At the Harmandir it is offered throughout the day, although the morning and evening are special times. In the Harmandir, people offer money so that *karah prasad* can be given out in their names.

Maharaja Ranjit Singh and his family are still mentioned because of the enormous grants they made for this.

For the rest of the day, unbroken readings (*akhand paths*) of the Guru Granth Sahib are

The Guru Granthi Sahib is carried back to its resting place on a palanquin.

The granthi *covers the holy book with cloths.*

carried out. Teams of readers take their turn until the book is finished.

Shifts of musicians then arrive. They sing and play for one-and-a-half hours each. Formal prayers are offered throughout the day at certain hours. The day ends at ten or eleven at night, when the evening *hukam* (verse) is taken from the bottom of the same left-hand page that was read from in the morning. A prayer is said before bed time. Then the *granthi* finally closes the holy book and wraps it in many splendid cloths.

Another *Ardas* is recited and the *granthi* puts the Guru Granth Sahib on his head, to show respect, and carries it to its palanquin. At one time, a procession then used to take the book back to the Akal Takht for the night. However, since the Akal Takht was damaged in 1984, the holy book is now taken to a temporary resting place while the Akal Takht is being rebuilt.

When the holy book is carried through the gates of the Harmandir, people throw rose petals to welcome it. The great drum, a kettle drum which is kept in all *gurdwaras*, is beaten as the book is carried. A special place is prepared for the book to rest for the night. After more prayers, everyone is given more *karah prasad* and then they go home.

At the Harmandir, work continues as preparations are made for the next day.

The gateway to the Harmandir, with silver gates.

The floors are washed and swept, and new carpets are spread out for people to sit on. Brooms made of peacock feathers are used for sweeping.

Life in other *gurdwaras*

The same routine is carried out in all *gurdwaras*. In town *gurdwaras* or village *gurdwaras*, the routine is a bit simpler than at the Harmandir. The Harmandir has many helpers but a village *gurdwara* might only have a *granthi* who opens and closes the book. People visit their *gurdwara* as and when they can during the working day. Sikhs believe that people should not make a rigid routine out of religion; pomp and ceremony are unnecessary. Leading a good life, getting married and having children, are the most important things.

Key words

palanquin a large box on poles, carried on people's shoulders

conch a large shell used as a trumpet

Maharaja a great prince

Seva – service to others

Seva – *washing the marble pavements around the Harmandir.*

Sikhs believe that it is very important to help people and to share with each other. Helping and sharing are shown through *seva*, which means 'service'. In any Sikh *gurdwara*, it is important to work together for the good of everybody. *Seva* includes sweeping the temple, looking after people's shoes when they take them off outside the *gurdwara*, and cooking.

Kar seva – cleaning the pool

In Amritsar, the problem of cleaning out the enormous pool at the Harmandir is solved through *kar seva*, which means 'work service'. The last two times that the pool was drained and cleaned were in 1923 and 1973. It is said that in 1973 over a million people came to help.

First, five people are chosen to lead the workforce. Sikhs believe that five is a special number because Guru Govind Singh chose five people to form the Khalsa (see page 11). Usually, five people are picked out to lead any activity. After the leaders are chosen to start the *kar seva*, they are given golden spades and silver bowls to begin digging out the mud at the bottom of the pool. Sikhs do not think that the mud is dirty. The fifth Guru, Arjan, once said that the mud in the sacred pool is like saffron, which is an expensive spice, the colour of gold.

Everyone else joins in with the work once the five leaders have scooped out the first few bowlfuls of sacred mud. In 1973, there were so many helpers that not all of them got a chance to carry the bowls of soil! While this

Working together to make chappatis *in the Guru's kitchen of the Bangla Sahib Gurdwara, Delhi.*

believe that eating together breaks down the barriers between people and unites them.

Today, in all *gurdwaras*, from the ancient ones in Amritsar to the smaller local ones in towns and cities all over the world, there is a *langar*. Meals are offered at any time and to anyone, no matter where they come from or what religion they observe. Everyone joins in with preparation of the food. This food is an offering to God.

A special holy food, *karah prasad*, is offered to people when they visit the *gurdwara* (see page 24). This can be made in the home or in the *langar*. But wherever it is made certain

enormous task takes place, the workers are given plenty of food and drink from the Guru's kitchen.

The Guru's kitchen

The early Gurus began the tradition of gathering visitors together for a meal. Everyone who came to visit the Gurus ate with them. Each Guru had his own *langar*, a kitchen with a canteen area nearby. Sikhs

Food being served at the Golden Temple.

Karah prasad being offered at the Harmandir.

rituals must be observed. The people who make the *karah prasad* must first take a bath and they must not wear their shoes in the kitchen. The kitchen itself is specially cleaned, together with the cooker and all the pots, pans and other kitchen tools. While the food is being cooked, *shabads* must be recited, and when it is taken to the *gurdwara*, the food is blessed with a *kirpan* (sword).

Karah prasad is a sweetmeat – a kind of *halva*. It is a mixture of semolina, sugar, water and butter. When this warm, sweet mixture is offered to Sikhs, they cup their hands to receive it and bow.

Temples and shrines

Amritsar has many other shrines and places of worship. Some belong to Hindus, Christians and Muslims. But most are visited by Sikhs, who come to worship God and to honour the lives and deaths of the Sikh Gurus and heroes.

Baba Dip Singh

A light always burns at the shrine of Baba Dip Singh. Baba Dip Singh was a scholar who

spent his life making copies of the Guru Granth Sahib, the Sikh holy scriptures (see pages 20-22). He lived in Amritsar during very troubled times. There were constant invasions from Afghanistan as the Muslim Emperor, Ahmad Shah, and his army pushed through the Panjab on their way to Delhi.

In 1757, Ahmad Shah blew up the Harmandir and filled the pool with the insides of dead cows. This was both a disaster and a dreadful insult to the Sikhs. Not only were their sacred temple and pool devastated, but also a highly respected animal had been slaughtered and dishonoured.

◄ *Visiting the shrine to Baba Dip Singh. Here, a light shines day and night.*

Flowers are laid on the spot where Baba Dip Singh died. ▼

Baba Dip Singh was outraged. He announced that he would fight the Muslims and rebuild the Harmandir, and then travelled around villages asking for support. In the end, about 5,000 villagers banded together under the command of Baba Dip Singh. They marched towards Amritsar to fight Ahmad Shah and his soldiers. On the way, most of the Sikhs were killed and Baba Dip Singh was wounded in the neck. He fought on for many miles until he reached the pathway around the sacred pool. Here, Baba Dip Singh lay down and died. Pilgrims place flowers on the spot where he lay, and a shrine has been built nearby.

Baba Atal Tower rises above most of the other buildings in Amritsar. Each of the nine floors represents a year in Atal Rai's short life.

Baba Atal

A tall tower rises above most other buildings in Amritsar. It is called Baba Atal and is named after Atal Rai, who was the son of Guru Hargovind. Atal Rai died when he was only nine years old, and this building reminds Sikhs of his story. It is said that before Atal Rai's death, one of his playmates had died and Atal Rai brought him back to life. The Gurus did not encourage their followers to believe in miracles, so Atal Rai's father could not approve of his son's action. Atal Rai then lay down and died to make up for his mistake. The tall tower of Baba Atal has nine floors – one for each year of the child's life.

Pools and trees

Sikhs do not only visit holy buildings in Amritsar. There are many other sites which are important to them, including several pools. Ramsar Pool is especially famous because Guru Arjan sat beside it to dictate the Guru Granth Sahib (see page 20).

Some of the very old trees in Amritsar are also special to Sikhs. Many people visit the trees under which Guru Arjan and Baba Buddha used to sit and teach (see page 35). Others gather around the tree where legend has it that Rajani left her sick husband in order to beg for food elsewhere (see page 34).

New towns

The Sikh religion moves forward all the time, changing with the demands of the modern world. Near Amritsar, at Beas, a new settlement has been built by Sikhs, Hindus and others. They follow a religious tradition called Radhasoami. The Radhasoamis explain religious teachings in a very simple way to the hundreds of people who visit Beas every year. The members of this group combine teaching with planning and running their well organized town. Visitors are shown around model farms, clinics that offer herbal cures, and a modern eye hospital.

Many mandirs

There are many Hindu *mandirs* (temples) to visit in Amritsar. One of these is Durgiana Mandir, which is very similar to the Harmandir. It was built in 1921. Other *mandirs*, such as Sitla Mandir, are hundreds of years old. Anyone who catches measles or chickenpox is brought to Sitla Mandir for a blessing. People of other faiths can worship in Amritsar, for there are also mosques and Christian churches.

▲ *Muslims praying at a mosque in Amritsar.*

The elaborate doorway of the Durgiana Mandir in
▼ *Amritsar.*

Saint Paul's Church, Amritsar.

Art and architecture

Some of the most spectacular art and architecture in Amritsar is found in the Golden Temple, although many of the styles can also be seen in other religious buildings and in ordinary homes throughout the city.

Ranjit Singh rebuilt the Harmandir in the early 19th century. It was he who had the building covered in gold and marble (see page 18). The main structure of the building is thought to be very much like that of the previous temple. Most of the new building was begun by the *misldars* (warlords) soon after the second temple had been destroyed. They tried to make it in the same design. But the finish and decoration of the Harmandir owe their beauty to Ranjit Singh and his team of artists and craftsmen.

The style of building and decoration used at this time in the Panjab is called 'Late Mughal'. This is probably because most of the artists and craftsmen had worked for the crumbling Muslim Mughal empire in the late 18th century. When the empire finally fell apart, these men took their skills with them to

▲ *Golden walls on the outside of the Harmandir.*

The Harmandir needs constant repair. Here, stonemasons
▼ *are carving big chunks of marble.*

other parts of the Panjab. Some craftsmen went to work at the courts of rulers in the Panjab hills. Other artisans took their skills to Ranjit Singh, who employed many craftsmen, including Sikhs and Hindus.

The Muslim architects brought many Islamic building traditions with them to India. Domes and arches were the most outstanding examples of Islamic influence. But other features were of older, Hindu styles. This mixture of Islamic and Hindu artistry produced an explosion of beauty which can be seen in the Harmandir today.

Looking at the Harmandir

A long, wide bridge leads across the sacred pool to the Golden Temple. A sundial rests halfway along the bridge. The roof of the temple itself has a large dome, shaped like a lotus flower. It is surrounded by smaller domes and tiny umbrella-shaped kiosks. The top part of the building is covered with a

The technique of ▶ shish mahal – *setting mirrored glass into the walls.*

Gold and rich colours decorate the ceiling on the first floor of the ▼ *Harmandir.*

▲ *Elephants inlaid into marble walls.*

◀ *Fruit inlays pattern the marble.*

layer of gleaming gold. At one time, people wanted to cover the Harmandir with solid gold, studded with precious jewels. But it was feared that the gold would be stolen, so copper and brass plates were attached to the outside walls and then **gilded**. It is said that there are 162 kilograms of gold altogether on the temple.

The lower part of the outside walls is covered with marble, which is **inlaid** with pictures of deer, elephants, birds, butterflies and many other animals. Flowers, and fruit such as bunches of grapes pattern the gleaming marble. The inlaid animals symbolize the struggles we face in this world, and the fruit and flowers depict the riches of life.

Gold and glass

Inside the Harmandir, the large hall is decorated with **filigree** and **enamel** work in gold. Above the hall there is a room that glistens and sparkles as you enter. Here,

A fresco in Baba Atal, showing the young Guru Nanak in a field of buffaloes (see page 9).

thousands of pieces of coloured, mirrored glass have been set into the walls. This technique is known as *shish mahal*, which means, 'palace of mirrors'.

Wood and plaster

Woodcarving has produced many intricate patterns on doors and **lintels** both in the Harmandir and in many ordinary homes throughout Amritsar. Beautiful effects have been achieved by using delicate inlays of different woods and ivory.

A different type of decoration was made with **plaster of Paris.** The mixture of powdered plaster and water had to be made up in very small amounts because it dries hard very quickly and then cannot be used. The soft plaster mixture was smoothed on to a wall and then scraped and carved into floral designs and lettering. Once the plaster had dried, colours and gold were added.

Frescoes

Frescoes are paintings made on damp plastered walls. These pictures were once very popular in Amritsar. Today, many people plaster or paint over the frescoes, but there are still some fine examples in the Harmandir of flowers and a small one of the Guru Govind Singh. The paintings on the walls of the Akal Takht were destroyed in 1984, but there are still some in the Baba Atal. The technique for making these particular frescoes is no longer used today. Paint was actually beaten into the walls. It was a very skilled job.

Key words

gilded   covered with a thin layer of gold

inlaid   patterned with shapes set into stone, wood or metal

filigree   fine lacework of gold or silver

enamel   a coating of coloured glass on metal

lintel   a long block of wood or stone over a doorway or window

plaster of Paris   soft, powdered mineral

Legends and traditions

There are many traditions associated with the founding of Amritsar and with nearby shrines (see pages 13-14). Countless stories are told of the Gurus and their friends.

Rajani of Patti

The 'Pool of Miracles' on which Amritsar now stands is surrounded in legend. Perhaps the best known and loved is the story of a girl called Rajani (say it as 'Raj-nee'), who came from the town of Patti. Rajani's father was a magistrate and a tax collector, and was respected by the whole community. He had five daughters, four of whom were already married and had left home. Rajani was the youngest and had no husband.

One day, the whole family went on an outing together. On the way home they met a group of holy saints who were praising God's Name. The four married daughters ignored the saints and went straight back home. But Rajani stayed to listen to the holy men singing a hymn by Guru Nanak, which was all about God's love for people.

When she returned home she told her sisters all about God's love for them. Rajani's father was furious. He told his daughters that it was he who had loved them and given them everything they had. Rajani replied that, on the contrary, everything was really a gift from God, and that God loves and protects us all.

After some time, a crippled man came to Patti. He had leprosy, which is a terrible disease. Rajani's father made her marry this poor man and then sent them both away without any wedding gifts or money.

Rajani spent many months praying to God for help, and begging for food. She is often pictured pushing her sick husband around in a cart. Some people say that she carried him in a basket. The poor man begged his wife to take him on pilgrimage to the holy sites, to find a cure for his illness. So Rajani took her husband all over India, hoping for a miracle.

One day, the couple arrived at a small pool, where Guru Amar Das had planned for a larger pool to be dug. Rajani left her husband under a tree that overhung the pool, and went to beg for some food. While she was gone, the sick man saw two large black crows fighting over a piece of bread which in the end fell into the pool. The birds swooped down into the water – and emerged as swans! Seeing this miracle, the poor man lowered himself into the water and came out completely cured and very handsome, except for one poor finger which he had kept above water to hold on to the tree that grew by the water's edge.

This now handsome man waited for his wife, who of course did not recognize her husband and refused to accept him. Some people from the nearby village advised Rajani to ask Guru Amar Das for his help. Rajani told the Guru the whole sad story, and of her fears that a strange man was trying to claim her as his wife!

The Guru listened patiently, and after he had heard the whole tale, he told Rajani that the pool was a place of supreme pilgrimage. Anyone who bathed there would be spiritually healed. The Guru then suggested that the husband should put his one bad finger into the pool. The husband did as he was asked and the finger was cured.

Rajani was overjoyed. Her husband thanked the Guru by helping him with his building programme. As for Rajani's father, he gave up all his wealth and spent the rest of his life following the Guru.

The tree by the pool still stands, and is a popular place of pilgrimage. It is called Dukhbhanjani Ber, which means, 'the ber tree that destroys sorrow'.

Baba Buddha

Baba Buddha was a great friend of many of the Gurus. There are a lot of stories about him. When he was a small boy, Baba Buddha used to sit by Guru Nanak and listen to his teachings. The Guru was surprised to see such a young child listening to him so intently. He told the boy that childhood was the time for sleeping, eating and playing, not for listening to a Guru's words. The young Baba Buddha replied that when his mother had told him to light a fire, he had noticed that it was the little twigs that got burned first. The boy thought that the little twigs represented young children like himself, and that he would die young. So it was important to him to listen carefully to the Guru now.

But the boy lived to be a very old man. He became so highly respected that he was given the duty of finding five of the Gurus. It is said that when he was searching for the third Guru, Amar Das, Baba Buddha let Amar Das's horse loose so that he could follow it home and find the next Guru. When Baba Buddha reached the house of Amar Das,

Baba Buddha advising Guru Arjan's wife.

there was a notice on the front door which read, 'To whoever opens this door, I am *not* his Guru, and he is not my Sikh!' Baba Buddha was not put off by this. As far as he was concerned, Amar Das was to be the next Guru. Baba Buddha was very polite and did not try to enter the door with the notice on it. Instead, to find his next Guru, he smashed a hole straight through the wall of the house!

Baba Buddha ber tree under which Baba Buddha sat.

Festivals and celebrations

All over the world, Sikhs take part in many different kinds of festival and celebration. Some festivals take place at the same time as ancient Hindu festivals; others are held to mark the births and deaths of the ten Gurus. These occasions are known as *gurpurbs*. Many Sikhs also remember the deaths of the Sikh martyrs. There are also family celebrations.

At most festivals in India, a fair known as a *mela* is held, with trading, various competitions and religious, social and political meetings. At *gurpurbs*, hundreds of people often parade through the streets to watch the magnificent Guru Granth Sahib being carried ceremoniously through the crowds. At the temple, an *akhand path*, a continuous reading of the holy scriptures, takes place (see page 22). Everyone gets together to eat at the *langar* (see page 27).

Vaisakhi festival

The Gurus encouraged Sikhs to gather together during three of the main Hindu festivals: Vaisakhi, Holi and Diwali. But the Gurus gave each of these festivals a special meaning for their own followers.

According to the Sikh calendar, Vaisakhi takes place on New Year's Day, in the middle of April. Vaisakhi is a festival of thanksgiving to God because it takes place just before harvest time. The festival is also special because on this day in 1699, Guru Govind Singh chose the members of the first Khalsa (see page 11). Now, new members of the Khalsa often join on New Year's day.

Vaisakhi is especially important in Amritsar. Sikhs began to gather in the city to celebrate this occasion during the 18th century. Now, many pilgrims flock to the

Sikhs gather at Anandpur for the Hola Mohalla festival.

Harmandir on the morning of Vaisakhi. They begin to arrive before dawn and stream in all day until late in the evening.

Political meetings take place in a part of the city called Jallianwala Bagh. Here, in 1919, British troops killed hundreds of Panjabis who had gathered together for New Year

In India, a young Sikh girl is talking about her faith at a gathering during Vaisakhi.

celebrations. The British ruled India at this time and felt that large meetings of Sikhs were a threat to them. Today, a *mela* is held near Jallianwala Bagh. Camels, goats and other animals are bought and sold, and everybody relaxes before the year's harvesting begins.

Hola Mohalla (Holi)

For Hindus in Amritsar and all over India, Holi is a celebration of springtime. People are strengthened and renewed spiritually. At Holi, everyone has a lot of fun, as they splash each other with coloured water and then dress up in their best clothes for a celebration.

But Guru Govind Singh also made Holi a special occasion for Sikhs. It became a day for training Sikh soldiers. Mock battles were held and competitions took place to find the best horsemen and swordsmen. The Guru renamed the festival *Hola Mohalla*, which means, 'attack and place of attack'. Today, Anandpur, to the east of Amritsar, is the only town which keeps the tradition of holding wrestling contests, and other competitions.

British Sikhs parading through the streets at Vaisakhi.

Diwali

Diwali is held in October and November, and is important to both Hindus and Sikhs. There are many stories associated with this festival. Hindus celebrate the time when the great king, Ram, and his queen, Sita, returned to their kingdom after many adventures, hardships and battles against evil. Diwali is

Marching with weapons at Hola Mohalla.

important to some people as the time when the goddess, Lakshmi, comes to Earth bringing wealth and good fortune. It is a time when light triumphs over darkness and when good overcomes evil.

At Diwali, Sikhs remember the time when Guru Hargovind was imprisoned by the Mughal emperor, Jehangir. When the Guru was offered his freedom, he asked whether his fellow prisoners could also be released. Guru Hargovind was told that he could bring out with him all the prisoners who managed to hold on to the Guru's clothes. So Guru Hargovind then asked for a special cloak with long tassles to be brought into the prison. Fifty-two prisoners held on to the special cloak and walked out as free men.

During Diwali, both Hindus and Sikhs light lamps – little baked clay bowls with a cotton wick inside, and filled with oil. The glowing lamps are placed all around the home, and coloured electric lights are often strung along the streets outside. Diwali is also party time, when sweets and other gifts are offered to friends and relatives. At night there are colourful firework displays.

▲ The martyr, Guru Tegh Bahadur, is remembered in this festival.

▼ This ceremony is being held to open a new Sikh temple in Kenya.

place every year on the day when the Guru Granth Sahib was first installed in the Harmandir (see page 20).

On all these days, a *jalau*, which means, 'a show of splendour', takes place. The treasures in the Golden Temple are put on display and the silver gates to the Harmandir are replaced with gold ones. Enormous amounts of food are prepared for the crowds of pilgrims. Lights are strung around the temple and fireworks brighten the night sky.

Birth and death

In Amritsar, special birthday celebrations take place for Guru Nanak, Guru Ram Das and Guru Govind Singh. A festival also takes

Think and do
1. Why do you think it is important that Sikhs and Hindus share some of their festivals? Describe and illustrate the festival that you would most like to see.   2. Diwali is a festival of light. Can you describe the importance of light in other festivals or religions?

A Sikh wedding is celebrated in a family home.

Around Amritsar

Amritsar was built in one of the richest parts of India, where people of different origins and faiths have mingled for many centuries. The city lies in the path of an ancient trade route to China and has stood in the way of invaders from Afghanistan, Central Asia and Persia. These traders and invaders left their mark on the ancient Hindu culture that had survived for centuries. More recently, Sikhs have brought ideas back to the area from America, Canada and many other countries, where Sikhs began to settle about 100 years ago. The result of all these influences can be seen in the rich culture and traditions of Amritsar.

The city dwellers live amongst both magnificent old buildings and practical modern shops, offices and flats. The old and new rub happily alongside each other, for Sikhs preserve tradition but also welcome progress. Many people live in spacious, modern homes made of patterned brickwork. Inside, the large rooms have fine furnishings, for Amritsar is quite a prosperous city

◀ *An art class at a Roman Catholic school in Amritsar.*

▼ *One of the many gates that leads into the city.*

Relaxing after school. Boys play with their spinning tops in the streets.

architecture, with intricate designs and patterns on the walls.

Clinics and hospitals can be found throughout the city, including a new hospital with a special Cancer Treatment Centre. This was opened in 1977 during the 400th anniversary celebrations of Amritsar.

Relaxing in Amritsar

Visitors to Amritsar will see many young people playing sports, especially hockey,

and its inhabitants enjoy making their homes beautiful.

Throughout the city there are many public buildings including schools and colleges, and Guru Nanak University. One of the colleges is called Khalsa College. It was founded in 1894 and was designed by Ram Singh, a well-known architect who had also worked on a room for the British Queen, Victoria. He developed a very lively style of

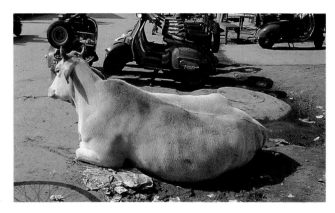

▲ *A cow rests on the side of the road.*

▼ *Making shoes in Amritsar.*

A shoe shop with rows of shiny sandals.

cricket and football, which are great favourites. Wrestling and a local game called *kabbadi* are also popular. The sky over the city is often patterned with bright kites, for kite-flying is an ancient and well-loved pastime. There is a lot of rivalry in this particular sport. Some people even stick ground glass on to their kite strings, to cut down someone else's as the kites jostle in the air!

Amritsar has many shopping areas to stroll around, from the modern Mall to the Katra Jaimal Singh and the old markets, such as the Bazaar Mai Sewan. Bright saris and the traditional patterned, curl-toed shoes

contrast with modern electrical gadgets and video sets.

After browsing in the shops and markets people like to eat out in the many cafés, restaurants and hotels. Children flock to the new ice-cream parlour, which stocks a dazzling choice of flavours.

Like most cities, Amritsar is studded with flower-filled parks and gardens. One of the best known gardens is Jallianwala Bagh, where hundreds of Sikhs were killed or wounded by British troops in 1919. In 1960, a monument called the Flame of Liberty was placed in the garden to remind people of the victims of the massacre.

Bullet holes in the archways of Jallianwalla Bagh gardens.

One of the many beautiful gardens in Amritsar.

This meal has spicy sauces, rice, yoghurt and salad.

Feeding a buffalo in the fields just outside Amritsar.

Eating in Amritsar

Amritsar is surrounded by rich farmland. Roads leading into the city cut through lush, green pasture and yellow mustard fields. The countryside is striped with irrigation channels. Dams in the hills provide water for the fields and electricity for the city. A fertile soil provides excellent conditions for grazing animals and growing food crops. Buffaloes, cows, chickens and pigs provide milk and meat for the people of Amritsar. A rich variety of cereals and vegetables, and fruits such as oranges, mangoes and bananas, are taken to the bustling market place of Amritsar, giving city dwellers exciting ingredients for their dishes.

A good way to start the day in Amritsar is by tucking into a flaky fried bread called *paratha*, with fried eggs and spicy pickles. At dinner time, many Sikhs eat only vegetable dishes, while others enjoy red meat, chicken and fish. Most main meals include fresh vegetables. A favourite dish is mustard leaves or spinach, with plenty of butter and corn bread. Rice is often served but most people prefer *chappati*, a round flat bread. A meal is often finished off with buttermilk and sweet rice pudding flavoured with almonds, fruits and cardamom.

Selling spices in a shop in Amritsar.

A changing city

Sikhism has changed constantly throughout its history, and especially during the last 100 years. Amritsar has often been a focus for these developments, as many different Sikh groups began and grew here.

Sikhs under British rule

British rule in India brought all kinds of changes to Amritsar. On the one hand, Indians were badly treated by the British, who were at times extremely brutal. On the other hand, many Panjabis were chosen to become soldiers in the British army. The colonial rulers also brought wealth to the city, new technology and western education. These three things enabled Sikhs to earn money and develop skills, but some Sikhs got badly into debt.

Because of these changes, a new group of Sikhs emerged, called the Akalis, after famous Sikh warriors of the 18th century. They wanted people to follow the strict code of the Khalsa (see page 11) and not be corrupted by money. The Akalis also wanted the *gurdwaras* to be managed properly. In 1920, their wish was granted, and the Shiromani Gurdwara Prabandhak Committee was formed to look after all places of worship.

Sikhism in India today

The struggles of nationalism and reform, and the partition of India into India and Pakistan, made many Sikhs very political, even after India gained independence in 1947. In the 1960s, the Sikh political party, the Akali Dal, struggled to gain a new state for Panjabi speakers. Even though the Akali Dal was granted their wish, there have been many other battles to win economic, religious and political rights for Sikhs.

These struggles led to a disaster for Amritsar in June 1984, as Indian security forces stormed the Harmandir area. In 1989, the Indian Prime Minister, Mrs Indira Gandhi, was killed by Sikh bodyguards. This has led to more conflict between different religious groups in India.

But today, the battered buildings in Amritsar are being restored, and it is hoped that it will once more be the jewel of the Panjab. On the streets, fighting has been stopped, and people now move around more freely. The future for Amritsar looks more settled than it has done for a long time. Sikhism is a religion of peace, truth, justice and equality, so it would be fitting if the holy city of Amritsar could follow a peaceful path.

Looking across the pool to the Harmandir.

Important events

The following are some important events with the dates on which they occurred:

AD THE YEARS AFTER THE BIRTH OF CHRIST: THE MODERN ERA

1469 Birth of Guru Nanak, the First Sikh Guru, at Nankana Sahib, Pakistan

1526–1858 India is under the rule of the Muslim Mughals

1539 Guru Angad becomes the second Guru

1552 Guru Amar Das becomes the third Guru. He establishes the site of Amritsar near the 'pool of miracles'

1574 Guru Ram Das becomes the fourth Guru. He begins to build Amritsar by having the pools dug out

1581 Guru Arjan becomes the fifth Guru. He lines the pools with bricks, and collects all the religious poems together. The Guru Granth Sahib (Sikh holy writings) is compiled at a place now known as Ath Sath Tirath

1606 Guru Hargovind becomes the sixth Guru. The Akal Takht is built

1644 Guru Har Rai becomes the seventh Guru

1661 Guru Har Krishan becomes the eighth Guru

1664 Guru Tegh Bahadur becomes the ninth Guru

1675 Govind Singh becomes the tenth and last Guru

1708 The last human Guru dies. The Guru Granth Sahib becomes the guide for all Sikhs

1757 Emperor Ahmad Shah and the Afghanistan army blow up the Harmandir

1770 Rebuilding the Harmandir begins

1776 The pool, Harmandir, bridge and gate to the Harmandir (Darshani Darwaza) are completed

1794 Jassa Singh Ramgarhia, a great Sikh leader, builds large *bunga* (residence) in Amritsar. Afterwards, many *bunga*s are built

1799 Maharaja Ranjit Singh, a great Sikh emperor, seizes Lahore

1800s The Harmandir is rebuilt with marble and gold. Amritsar grows

1839 Death of Maharaja Ranjit Singh

1846 The British fight the Sikh army

1849 British gain control of the Panjab

1894 Khalsa College is founded

1919 Killing of Sikhs by British troops at Jallianwala Bagh

1920 Formation of Shiromani Gurdwara Prabandhak Committee, which manages the *gurdwaras*

1923 The pool at the Harmandir is drained and cleaned

1947 India and Pakistan are declared separate states. Amritsar lies in India, but other holy sites connected with Guru Nanak remain in Pakistan, which has a largely Muslim population. India gains independence from Britain

1973 The pool at the Harmandir is drained and cleaned again

1984 Indian troops storm the Harmandir area and some of the buildings get damaged. There is a lot of unrest

1990s Amritsar becomes more settled and peaceful. Damaged buildings are restored

Further Reading

Listening to Sikhs Olivia Bennett (Unwin Hyman)
Growing up in Sikhism Andrew Clutterbuck (Longman Group)
The Sikh World Daljit Singh and Angela Smith (Macdonald)

The Founders of Sikh Religion Jagdish Singh (Guru Nanak Foundation, New Dehli)
The Sikhs and their way of life Gurinder Singh Sacha (Sikh Missionary Society)

Index

Sikhism
India